Colorado hiking

HIKES IN

COLORADO

2024

Unlock and discover the captivating trail, natural Paradise, untamed beauty, the hidden jewels, across the stunning landscapes of Colorado.

Larry Lawler

TABLE OF CONTENTS

1. INTRODUCTION

We would like to take this opportunity to welcome you to the Colorado Hiking Guide 2024, your reliable companion for travel across the stunning landscapes of Colorado. With the help of this book, we will set off on an adventure to see the varied and breathtaking landscapes that make Colorado a paradise for hikers. Let's get ready to go on an exciting journey, shall we? Put on your boots, get your rucksack and get ready to plunge in!

1.1 Purpose of the Guide

If you want to have a hiking experience in Colorado that you will never forget, our goal with this book is to be the resource you refer to the most. This book is designed to give you trial insights, suggestions, and recommendations that will guarantee your time spent on the trails is nothing short of exceptional. Whether you are an experienced hiker or a newbie who is ready to explore, we have developed this guide to meet your needs.

1.2 About Colorado's Diverse Terrain

The Rocky Mountains, wide plains, and high desert plateaus are just some of the landscapes that can be seen in Colorado, which is sometimes referred to as the Centennial State. Colorado is home to an unrivaled range of geographical features. In this part, we dig into the geological marvels that await you, providing a glance into the various traits that make each location a special tapestry of natural beauty.

From the towering peaks of the Rockies, whose snow-capped summits reach for the sky, to the red rock canyons and mesas of the southwest, Colorado's topography is a playground for outdoor enthusiasts. We'll accompany you through the varied habitats, emphasizing the rich biodiversity and spectacular treasures that await discovery on the trails.

1.3 Safety Tips and Guidelines

Your safety is our top concern. Before going out on your Colorado hiking experience, take the time to educate yourself with some critical safety tips:

1. Know Your Limits:

Respect your fitness level and select paths that match your ability. Colorado provides treks for all abilities, so you're likely to find one that fits you.

2. Check the Weather:

Colorado weather may be unpredictable. Be prepared for rapid variations in temperature, particularly at higher altitudes. Pack layers and keep updated about the forecast.

3. Stay Hydrated:

The height and dry air might contribute to dehydration. Carry an ample amount of water and drink continuously during your trip.

4. Wildlife Awareness:

Colorado is home to various animals. Keep a safe distance, particularly around bigger animals like elk and moose. Familiarize oneself with fundamental animal behavior.

5. Leave No Trace:

Preserve the beauty of Colorado by adopting Leave No Trace principles. Pack out all your waste, remain on approved paths, and respect the environment.

6. Emergency Preparedness:

Carry a basic first aid kit, know your location, and advise someone of your trekking intentions. In case of an emergency, be cool and ask for aid.

As we go on our excursion together, remember that ethical hiking assures not only your safety but also the preservation of Colorado's magnificent nature. Now, let's dig into the heart of Colorado's trails, where every stride is a moment to appreciate and a link to the natural beauties that characterize this wonderful state.

2. PLANNING YOUR HIKE

Congratulations on opting to experience the marvels of Colorado's trails! Before you hit the pathways, let's dig into the fundamental parts of organizing your trek. With the correct planning, your travel will be not simply fun but also safe and memorable.

2.1 Choosing the Right Trail

Colorado provides a variety of paths appealing to diverse interests and fitness levels. Let's break down how to find the best path for you:

Terrain Type:

Mountain routes: If you seek panoramic vistas and clean mountain air, choose routes in the Rockies.

Desert Hikes: For a flavor of the southwest, explore paths through red rock canyons and mesas.

Plains & Plateaus: If you want a softer landscape, choose paths in the eastern plains or high desert plateaus.

Difficulty Level:

Easy Trails: Perfect for novices or those wanting a calm walk.

Moderate Trails: A bit of a struggle, appropriate for hikers with some experience.

Difficult Trails: Tailored for seasoned hikers, including steep ascents and difficult terrain.

Trail Length:

Short Hikes: Ideal for a half-day trip.

Day Hikes: Longer hikes are excellent for a full day of exploring.

Multi-Day Hikes: For the enthusiastic hiker, go on an overnight trip while camping along the route.

2.2 Seasonal Considerations

Colorado's seasons paint the terrain with a variety

of colors, each delivering a distinct hiking experience. Let's take a deeper look:

Spring:

Wildflowers in Bloom: Many pathways offer a spectacular display of wildflowers.

Moderate Temperatures: Comfortable weather for trekking, but be prepared for some residual snow at higher altitudes.

Summer:

Peak Hiking Season: Trails are often snow-free, allowing great hiking conditions.

Warmer Temperatures: Pack sunscreen and remain hydrated as the sun may be harsh.

Fall:

Changing Colors: Witness the aspen trees turn into a golden display.

Cooler Temperatures: Enjoy fresh, cold air as

you explore the trails.

Winter:

Snowy paths: Some paths are accessible with adequate clothing for winter trekking.

Snow Sports: Try snowshoeing or cross-country skiing on designated winter pathways.

2.3 Permits and Regulations

Before you leave on your vacation, let's examine the bureaucratic side of things — permits and rules. It's not as daunting as it sounds!

Permits:

Check Requirements: Some trails may need permits, particularly for overnight visits.

Reservations: If permits are required, get them in advance, particularly during high seasons.

Regulations:

Stay on Trails: Protect the environment by adhering to authorized trails.

Campsite Rules: Follow Leave No Trace principles while camping, and stick to specified campsites.

2.4 Gear Checklist

Now, let's make sure you're well-equipped for your excursion. Here's a checklist to ensure you have all the essentials:

Clothing:

Weather-Appropriate Layers: Dress in layers for shifting situations.

Sturdy Hiking Boots: Comfortable footwear is vital.

Gear:

Backpack: Choose one with ample space for necessities.

Navigation Tools: Map, compass, and/or GPS for route navigation.

Safety Items:

First Aid Kit: Basic materials for mild injuries.

Emergency Whistle: A simple yet powerful instrument for communication.

Nutrition and Hydration:

Water Bottles: Stay hydrated with a sufficient water supply.

Snacks: Pack energy-boosting snacks to keep you fuelled.

Weather Protection:

Rain Jacket: Be prepared for unexpected rain showers.

Sun Protection: Sunscreen, sunglasses, and a cap

for UV protection.

Miscellaneous:

Multi-Tool or Knife: Handy for numerous jobs.

Headlamp/Flashlight: Essential for low-light circumstances.

Now that you're equipped with the information to plan your trek like an expert, get ready to go on a memorable trip across the magnificent landscapes of Colorado. Happy trails!

3. TOP HIKING DESTINATIONS

Welcome to the crown jewels of Colorado's hiking landscape! In this segment, we'll unveil the mysteries of two legendary destinations: Rocky Mountain National Park and Maroon Bells-Snowmass Wilderness. These natural treasures offer a kaleidoscope of scenery that will leave you in awe. So, tighten your bootlaces, and let's explore these lovely hiking havens.

3.1 Rocky Mountain National Park

Nestled in the heart of Colorado, Rocky Mountain

National Park is a hiker's dream, where towering peaks, alpine lakes, and varied animals await. Let's explore the wonderful elements that make this park a must-visit place.

Trail Highlights:

Bear Lake Trail: A lovely and family-friendly circle around the magnificent Bear Lake, affording amazing views of Hallett Peak.

Sky Pond walk: For the brave, this walk takes you through lush meadows and past three lovely alpine lakes, concluding at the spectacular Sky Pond.

Scenic Vistas:

Trail Ridge Road: A picturesque journey exhibiting the park's different habitats, from montane forests to alpine tundra.

Chasm Lake Overlook: Marvel at the magnificent vistas of Longs Peak and the Diamond Face.

Wildlife Encounters:

Elk and Moose: Keep your eyes open for these gorgeous animals wandering the meadows.

Bighorn Sheep: Spot these distinctive Rocky Mountain dwellers ascending the high rocks.

Seasonal Tips:

Wildflower Extravaganza: Late spring and early summer offer a rush of wildflowers, changing the environment into a brilliant painting.

Snowy Wonders: Winter brings up possibilities for snowshoeing and cross-country skiing on approved pathways.

3.2 Maroon Bells-Snowmass Wilderness

Prepare to be charmed by the timeless splendor of Maroon Bells-Snowmass Wilderness. Renowned for its famous Maroon Bells peaks and stunning alpine lakes, this wilderness region is a mesmerizing location for trekkers seeking unsurpassed natural beauty.

Must-Explore Trails:

Maroon Lake Scenic Trail: A leisurely hike giving postcard-perfect vistas of the Maroon Bells reflected in the crystal-clear Maroon Lake.

Crater Lake Trail: A fairly tough climb leads to the magnificent Crater Lake, hidden behind the spectacular Maroon Bells.

Photographer's Paradise:

Maroon Lake daybreak: Capture the first light lighting the Maroon Bells for a stunning daybreak experience.

Snowmass Lake Reflections: Fall in love with the reflected reflections of Snowmass Mountain in the tranquil Snowmass Lake.

Backpacking Adventures:

Four Pass Loop: A tough yet rewarding multi-day

trip, ringing the Maroon Bells and conquering four high mountain passes.

Buckskin Pass: Revel in magnificent vistas as you rise to the picturesque Buckskin Pass.

Seasonal Delights:

Fall Foliage Spectacle: Autumn paints the aspen groves in colors of gold, producing a captivating scene.

Winter Tranquility: Experience the calm splendor of snow-covered peaks and frozen mountain lakes throughout the winter months.

As you venture into these trekking wonderlands, be prepared to be absorbed in the raw beauty of nature. Rocky Mountain National Park and Maroon Bells-Snowmass Wilderness entice with routes that offer not simply physical adventure but a spiritual connection to the soul-stirring vistas of Colorado. Lace up, take in the mountain air, and let the experience unfold.

3.3 Garden of the Gods

Welcome to the captivating Garden of the Gods, a natural sanctuary nestled away in Colorado Springs. This fascinating site is a geological wonder, where towering red rock formations and bright landscapes provide a surreal playground for hikers and wildlife lovers alike.

Unique Formations:

Kissing Camels: Marvel at the renowned rock formation depicting two camels enjoying a kiss, a wonderful picture destination.

Balanced Rock: Witness the natural equilibrium of a gigantic red rock defying gravity.

Hiking Trails:

Siamese Twins Trail: A modest climb leads to a natural window with amazing views of Pikes Peak.

Perkins Central Garden Trail: A simple hike

offers a close-up view of the different rock formations.

Rock Climbing Opportunities:

North Gateway Rock: Challenge yourself with rock climbing routes appropriate for all ability levels.

South Gateway Rock: Enjoy panoramic views of the park from the summit after a satisfying trek.

Photography Hotspots:

Sunset at High Point: Capture the bright colors as the sun sets behind the famed red rocks.

Steamboat Rock Reflections: Visit the Siamese Twins early morning for reflections of Steamboat Rock in the calm waters.

Visitor Center:

Interactive displays: Explore the Visitor Center for interesting displays about the park's geology and history.

Guided Nature hikes: Join pak rangers for guided hikes to learn more about the distinctive flora and animals.

3.4 Great Sand Dunes National Park and Preserve

Prepare to be astounded as we go to the strange vistas of the Great Sand Dunes National Park and Preserve. This remarkable resort mixes towering dunes with stunning mountain backgrounds, giving a unique outdoor experience.

Tallest Dunes in North America:

Star Dune: Climb to the summit of Star Sand, the handset dune in North America, for panoramic views of the surrounding mountains and sand fields.

High Dune: A somewhat less arduous hike with equally excellent sights.

Medano Creek Beach:

Seasonal Oasis: In late spring and early summer, Medano Creek produces a beach-like oasis at the foot of the dunes.

Sandcastle Building: Embrace your inner kid and construct sandcastles by the creek's side.

Adventure Activities:

Sand Sledding: Experience the exhilaration of sledging down the sandy slopes with rented sandboards or sledges.

Backcountry Exploration: Venture into the preserve's different habitats, from grasslands to wetlands.

Stargazing Opportunities:

Dune Star Observatory: On certain nights, join rangers for stargazing programmes beneath the dark sky of the park.

Night Photography: Capture the bizarre beauty of the dunes beneath the starry night sky.

Seasonal Considerations:

Summer Heat: Plan treks in the morning or evening to escape the severe noon heat.

Winter Tranquility: Experience the tranquil beauty of snow-covered dunes throughout the winter months.

As you tour the Garden of the Gods and the Great Sand Dunes National Park and Preserve, you're in for a visual feast of different landscapes. From the red rock formations of Colorado Springs to the surreal dunes in the Sangre de Cristo Mountains, these sites provide a tapestry of natural beauties that will etch unique memories into your adventurous spirit. So, let's continue on this adventure, where every step draws you closer to the stunning beauty of Colorado's different terrains.

4. TRAIL PROFILES

Embarking on a hiking excursion means knowing the lay of the ground, very literally. In this part, we'll uncover the subtleties of trail profiles, letting you find the optimal course that corresponds with your talents and time limits. So, let's dig into the realm of route difficulties, ratings, length, and expected duration to make your hiking trip as fun and rewarding as possible.

4.1 Difficulty Levels and Trail Ratings

Choosing the Right Difficulty:

Easy Trails (Green): These are suitable for beginners and casual hikers. Expect well-marked trails with moderate elevation rise, providing for a comfortable walk.

Moderate Trails (Blue): Ideal for those seeking a bit of a challenge. You could encounter tougher areas and rougher terrain, but the overall experience is still accessible for most hikers.

Difficult paths (Black): Geared towards seasoned hikers, these paths frequently require steep ascents, harsh terrain, and sometimes hard circumstances. Proper planning and experience are crucial.

Trail Ratings:

Understanding trail ratings may make your

decision-making process smoother. Ratings often incorporate elements like topography, elevation gain, and trail conditions. Here's a breakdown:

1-3: Easy hikes suited for most people.

4-6: Moderate trails that may contain steeper portions.

7-9: Difficult paths with hard terrain and sometimes dangerous circumstances.

10: Extremely tough trails, sometimes needing technical skills and harsh circumstances.

Before you head out, examine your fitness level, experience, and the trail rating to guarantee a safe and pleasant trip.

4.2 Length and Estimated Time

Trail Length:

The length of a route is an important aspect of planning your journey. Here's a short guide to various path lengths:

Short Hikes (1-3 miles): Perfect for a short excursion or those new to hiking.

Day Hikes (3-10 miles): Longer routes that may be done in a day, giving a more immersive experience.

Long Hikes (10+ miles): Multi-day activities for people wanting a prolonged relationship with nature.

Estimated Time:

Understanding how long a trek could take helps you organize your day successfully. Keep in mind that individual spaces may differ, but here's a rough guide:

Short Hikes: 1-2 hours

Day Hikes: 3-6 hours

Long Hikes: Dependent on distance, might vary from a whole day to several days.

Factors including height gain, terrain difficulties, and your fitness level impact hiking pace. It's usually a good idea to start early, particularly on longer walks, to provide adequate time to appreciate the surroundings and return safely.

By knowing difficulty levels, trail ratings, length, and expected duration, you'll be ready to pick the best path for your excursion. Now, let's strap on those boots and explore the different vistas that lie along the routes of Colorado's trails.

4.3 Elevation Gain and Loss

Welcome to the elevation rollercoaster of hiking paths! Understanding elevation gain and loss is like reading the topographical language of the wide outdoors. In this part, we'll unveil the secrets of rising peaks and lowering valleys to guarantee you're prepared for the ups and downs of your hiking experience.

Elevation Gain:

Gradual Incline: Trails with low elevation rise give a smooth start to uphill parts. Perfect for novices and those wanting a leisurely pace.

Moderate Climb: Expect a more perceptible incline. These paths test your endurance but provide great vistas as you gain height.

Steep Uphill: Strap in for a difficult ascent. Steeper slopes involve more work but can lead to beautiful panoramas at the peak.

Elevation Loss:

Gradual Decline: Trails with modes-drops provide for enjoyable treks. Your knees will appreciate you, and you can enjoy the beauty without worrying about severe dips.

Moderate Descent: A regulated downhill travel, somewhat steeper than a leisurely drop. Take your time and absorb the trail's intricacies.

Steep Downhill: Brace yourself for a steeper drop. Pay attention to footing and use trekking poles if required. The descent may be painful on the knees.

Strategies for Elevation Changes:
Pacing: Adjust your pace depending on the terrain. Conserve energy on uphills and retain control on downhills.

Hydration: Altitude may impact hydration. Drink water often, particularly on ascents, to counterbalance the increased effort.

Rest pauses: Take pauses wisely, especially on steep ascents. Resting enables your body to acclimatize to the difference in altitude.

4.4 Notable Features and Scenic Points

Get ready to be fascinated by the treasures that dot the pathways. As we explore Colorado's landscapes, we'll highlight the important features and beautiful locations that convert a trek into an amazing trip.

Rock Formations:
Red Rock Amphitheater: Marvel at the geological marvels created by time and weathering.

Hoodoos: Encounter enormous spires of rock, formed by erosion into fanciful structures.

Water Features:
Waterfalls: Discover secret waterfalls tumbling down rock sides, providing calm and pleasant locations along the walk.

Alpine Lakes: Reflecting the grandeur of surrounding peaks, alpine lakes are great for a tranquil rest and a magnificent picture op.

Panoramic Vistas:

Peak Views: Reach the peak for 360-degree vistas of the surrounding region.

Scenic Overlooks: Pause at designated views giving broad panoramas of valleys, canyons, and distant peaks.

Unique Flora and Fauna:

Wildflower Meadows: Be engulfed in a burst of hues throughout spring and summer as wildflowers carpet the meadows.

Animal Habitats: Keep a lookout for animal habitats, from birding places to locations frequented by bigger creatures.

Historical Points of Interest:

Mining Ruins: Explore relics of Colorado's mining heritage, with abandoned buildings narrating stories of the past.

Native American locations: Some paths have locations important to Native American history, giving a cultural dimension to your journey.

Sunrise and Sunset Spots:

Early Morning Views: Experience the majesty of the first light as the sun rises over the mountains.

Dusk Delights: Stay for a beautiful sunset, painting the sky in shades of orange, pink, and purple.

As you explore the paths, each remarkable feature

and picturesque point adds a layer of enchantment to your hiking experience. So, let's journey out, where every step gets you closer to the mesmerizing scenery and distinctive characteristics that make Colorado's trails a tapestry of natural beauty.

5. HIKING WITH KIDS AND PETS

Embarking on a family excursion or taking your pet buddies along for the trek adds a whole new depth to the trail experience. In this complete guide, we'll examine family-friendly routes, give ideas for hiking with youngsters, and dig into pet-friendly trails and restrictions. So, whether you're teaching your tiny ones to the marvels of nature or bringing your four-legged buddies along, let's make every step a pleasant one.

5.1 Family-Friendly Trails
Easy Adventures for All Ages
1. Bear Lake Trail (Rocky Mountain National Park):

Highlights: A picturesque circle around Bear Lake with a moderate elevation increase, excellent for strollers.

Family Fun: Educational signage along the route teaches youngsters about local animals and plant life.

2. Sprague Lake Trail (Rocky Mountain National Park):

Highlights: An easy loop around Sprague Lake with great mountain vistas.

Family Fun: Picnic spots by the lake offer a nice setting for a family picnic.

3. Wildflower Loop Trail (Garden of the Gods):

Highlights: A simple circle showing brilliant wildflowers and famous rock structures.

Family Fun: Interactive events at the Visitor Center engage youngsters in the marvels of the park.

4. Montezuma Well Trail (Great Sand Dunes

National Park):

Highlights: A brief circle examining the unusual geological characteristics near Montezuma Well.

Family Fun: Ranger-led events teach youngsters about the area's rich heritage.

5. Lily Lake Trail (Rocky Mountain National Park):

Highlights: An easy loop around Lily Lake with wonderful views of the surrounding mountains.

Family Fun: Opportunities for birding and animal viewing throughout the walk.

5.2 Tips for Hiking with Children

Making Family Hikes a Breeze

1. Plan Shorter Routes:

Kids have shorter attention spans, so pick routes that can be finished within a few hours.

2. Pack Snacks and Water:

Keep the energy levels up with a bag loaded with kid-friendly food and lots of water.

3. Bring Comfortable Gear:

Ensure your tiny ones have comfortable footwear, adequate attire, and maybe a hat for sun protection.

4. Create a Scavenger Hunt:

Keep youngsters involved by turning the trek into a treasure hunt. Look for certain flora, animals, or natural characteristics.

5. Take Breaks:

Plan for stops along the walk, enabling youngsters to relax, explore, and enjoy the environment.

6. Educate and Explore:

Share intriguing information about the environment, plants, and animals to make the journey an educational excursion.

7. Safety First:

Teach youngsters about trail safety, including keeping on the route, avoiding strange plants, and appreciating animals from a distance.

5.3 Pet-Friendly Trails and Regulations Adventures for Furry Companions

1. Elk Meadow Park (Evergreen):

Pet Perks: Off-leash pathways in selected regions, allowing wide spaces for dogs to explore.

Regulations: Leash regulations may vary, so be careful of signs and respect park standards.

2. Red Rock Canyon Open Space (Colorado Springs):

Pet Perks: Leashed dogs are permitted on the various pathways snaking through red rock formations.

Regulations: Respect leash regulations and pack away pet waste.

3. Garden of the Gods (Colorado Springs):

Pet Perks: Leashed dogs are permitted on specified paths.

Regulations: Follow leash restrictions and be careful of designated pet-friendly locations.

4. Chatfield State Park (Littleton):

Pet Perks: The park has a separate off-leash dog area for canine pals to play.

Regulations: Respect leash restrictions outside the designated off-leash area.

5. White Ranch Open Space (Golden):

Pet Perks: Leashed dogs may explore a network of pathways with their owners.

Regulations: Adhere to leash restrictions and be

mindful of any seasonal trail closures.

Pet-Friendly Hiking Tips

1. Leash Etiquette:

Keep your dog on a leash except in approved off-leash zones. This safeguards the safety of animals, other hikers, and your pet.

2. Pack Essentials:

Bring water, a dish, and waste bags for your pet. Responsible pet ownership is vital to keeping a clean and pleasant route.

3. Know Your Dog's Limits:

Consider your dog's fitness level and select paths that coincide with their ability. Steep or rocky routes may not be appropriate for all dogs.

4. Be Mindful of Wildlife:

Keep a safe distance from animals, and prevent your pet from upsetting local creatures.

5. Check Trail Regulations:

Before venturing out, learn particular trail restrictions regarding dogs. Some paths may have seasonal limitations or leash requirements.

By discovering family-friendly routes, following advice for hiking with children, and navigating pet-friendly trails properly, you'll create unique outdoor experiences for every member of your hiking group. Now, let's begin on pathways where the laughing of children and the joyful panting of dogs combine nicely with the rustling leaves and gentle winds of Colorado's stunning landscapes.

6. WILDERNESS SURVIVAL SKILLS

Welcome to the arena of wilderness survival skills, where your knowledge and readiness become the key to a safe and fun outdoor trip. In this lengthy book, we'll study key skills ranging from navigation and map reading to first aid basics, coping with animal encounters, and adopting the Leave No Trace ideals. So, buckle your metaphorical seatbelt, and let's travel through the foundations of surviving and flourishing in the wilderness.

6.1 Navigation and Map Reading
Navigating the Great Outdoors
1. Understanding Topographic Maps:

Features: Topographic maps illustrate elevation, landscape, and major features. Learn to understand contour lines, symbols, and scale.

2. Using a Compass:

Orientation: Understand how to align a compass with a map, and use it to locate your direction.

Bearings: Learn how to take and follow bearings for precise navigation.

3. Recognizing Landmarks:

Natural and Man-Made: Identify significant features including mountains, rivers, and unusual plants. Man-made landmarks, such as cottages or bridges, enhance navigation.

4. GPS Navigation:

Technology: Embrace the advantages of GPS gadgets. Learn to enter waypoints, follow tracks, and comprehend GPS coordinates.

5. Trail Markers and Signs:

Understanding: Familiarize yourself with trail

markings and signage. They steer you down set courses.

6. Emergency Navigation:

Terrain Association: Use nearby features to navigate if you lose your map or GPS.

6.2 First Aid Basics

Keeping Safe on the Trail

1. First Aid Kit Essentials:

Contents: Ensure your package contains bandages, antiseptic wipes, painkillers, adhesive tape, and any essential personal prescriptions.

2. Wound Care:

Cleaning: Clean cuts and wounds with sterile treatments or clean water. Use antiseptic wipes.

Dressing: Apply suitable dressings and bind them with bandages.

3. Treating Blisters:

Prevention: Use moleskin for blister pads on hotspots to avoid blisters.

Treatment: If blisters occur, clean and cover them with blister bandages.

4. Dealing with Sprains and Strains:

R.I.C.E. Method: Rest, Ice, Compression, Elevation. Follow this strategy for injuries to lessen swelling and promote recuperation.

5. Recognizing Signs of Dehydration:

Symptoms: Headache, dizziness, and dark urine are indicators of dehydration. Drink water consistently and notice the early indications.

6. CPR and Basic Life Support:

Training: Consider taking a CPR and basic life support course. Knowing these abilities may be helpful in crises.

6.3 Dealing with Wildlife Encounters

Sharing the Wilderness with Wildlife

1. Understanding Animal Behavior:

Observation: Learn about the habits of animals in the region you're investigating.

Indicators: Recognize indicators of animal activity, such as tracks or droppings.

2. Avoiding Encounters:

Noise: Make noise as you trek to notify animals of your presence.

Food Storage: Keep food securely secured to prevent attracting animals to your campground.

3. Responding to Encounters:

Stay Calm: If you meet animals, keep calm and prevent unexpected movements.

Back Away gently: Create space by backing away

gently without turning your back on the animal.

4. Bear Safety:

Bear Spray: Carry bear spray and know how to use it.

Bear Awareness: Understand bear behavior and practice bear safety measures in bear habitat.

5. Snakes and Insects:

Observation: Watch where you tread to avoid snakes. Be careful near nests of stinging insects.

First Aid: Know basic first aid for snake bites and bug stings.

6.4 Leave No Trace Principles

Preserving Nature for Future Generations

1. Plan Ahe Prepare:

Research: Know the legislation and weather

conditions for your location.

Minimal Impact Camping: Choose established campgrounds and utilize sturdy surfaces to reduce impact.

2. Travel and Camp on Durable Surfaces:

Stick to routes: Stay on designated routes to conserve delicate plants.

Campsite Selection: Choose existing campgrounds to decrease damage to the environment.

3. Dispose of Waste Properly:

Pack It Out: Carry out all rubbish, including food leftovers and litter.

Human Waste: Use existing bathroom facilities or the correct methods for digging cat holes.

4. Leave What You Find:

Natural Features: Avoid plucking flora or upsetting animals.

Historical items: Leave historical or cultural items unharmed.

5. Minimize Campfire Impact:

Consider Alternatives: Use a camp stove for cooking instead of creating a fire.

Fire Safety: If fires are authorized, practice Leave No Trace guidelines for appropriate campfire usage.

6. Respect Wildlife:

Observe from a Distance: Keep a safe distance from animals to prevent stress and disruption.

No Feeding: Do not feed wildlife; it interrupts their normal behavior and may be hazardous.

7. Be Considerate of Other Visitors:

Noise: Keep noise levels down to enable people to enjoy the sounds of nature.

Yielding: Yield to those on the route and be friendly to other hikers.

Congratulations on diving into the art of outdoor survival skills! By refining these qualities, you not only secure your safety but also help to the preservation of our natural environments. So, let's walk out with confidence, respecting the earth, knowing the fauna, and leaving just footprints behind as we explore the spectacular vistas of the great outdoors.

7. TRAIL CONSERVATION AND STEWARDSHIP

Welcome to the core of ethical outdoor adventure – trail protection and care. In this lengthy book, we'll dig into the significance of conservation, examine volunteering possibilities, and define ethical hiking methods. By learning and accepting these values, you become a protector of the trails, safeguarding their beauty and accessibility for centuries to come.

So, let's go on this path of environmental care and ethical outdoor adventure.

7.1 Importance of Conservation
Preserving Nature's Masterpieces
1. Biodiversity Preservation:

Ecosystem Health: Trails typically span varied environments. By protecting these ecosystems, we conserve the multitude of plant and animal species that call them home.

2. Erosion Prevention:
Route Impact: Proper route design and upkeep reduce erosion caused by foot traffic, ensuring the landscape stays intact.

3. Water Quality Protection:
Runoff Impact: Conserving trails may be maintained bitterly by minimizing soil erosion that

may contribute to runoff contamination in neighboring water bodies.

4. Cultural and Historical Heritage:

Reservation: Many paths retain historical and cultural importance. Conservation activities conserve objects and locations, preserving our common legacy.

5. Scenic Beauty for Future Generations:

Visual Impact: Conserving paths guarantees that future generations may enjoy the same awe-inspiring beauty that draws us now.

6. Minimizing Human-Wildlife Conflict:

Respectful Practices: Conservation practices assist preserve a balance that avoids harmful human effects on animal habitats, decreasing confrontations.

7.2 Volunteering Opportunities

Contributing to Trail Preservation

1. Trail Maintenance Teams:

Regular Maintenance: Join organizations that spend on time tontrail maintenance, fixing erosion damage, cleaning debris, and ensuring trails stay safe.

2. Habitat Restoration Projects:

Invasive Species Removal: Participate in efforts to eradicate invasive plant species that endanger native flora.

3. Educational Programs:

Guided Nature Walks: Volunteer as a guide for nature walks, informing tourists about local flora, animals, and conservation techniques.

4. Adopt-a-Trail Programs:

Personal Responsibility: Adopt a particular path and accept responsibility for its care, from frequent cleaning to reporting difficulties.

5. Community Cleanup Initiatives:

Trash Removal: Engage in community-led cleaning programmes to remove trash from trails and adjacent areas.

6. Trail Building Projects:

Sustainable Design: Join trail-building teams to develop trails with little environmental effect, using erosion control methods.

7. Wildlife Monitoring:

Citizen Science: Contribute to wildlife monitoring programs, gathering data and supporting apps in conservation efforts.

7.3 Responsible Hiking Practices

Treading Lightly on the Trails

1. Stay on Designated Trails:

Trail Erosion: Straying from established trails may lead to erosion. Stick to existing pathways to minimize harm.

2. Leave No Trace:

Pack It In, Pack It Out: Carry out all rubbish, including food scraps and litter. Leave natural and cultural elements as finding them.

3. Respect Wildlife:

Observation from a Distance: Avoid approaching or feeding animals. Observe from a distance to decrease stress.

4. Avoid Trail Cutting:

Switchbacks: Follow switchbacks and avoid

cutting corners, since this may lead to erosion and harm plants.

5. Camp Responsibly:

Campsite Selection: Choose existing campgrounds to reduce damage. Follow Leave No Trace guidelines regarding fire usage.

6. Practice Fire Safety:

Fire restrictions: If fires are authorized, observe specified restrictions. Use designated fire rings and properly extinguish flames before leaving.

7. Respect Private Property:

Borders: Respect private property borders. Stick on established public paths and prevent trespassing.

8. Educate Others:

Share Knowledge: Spread knowledge about appropriate hiking methods. Educate other hikers on the need for conservation.

9. Be Mindful of Noise:

Natural Soundscape: Keep noise levels down to enable people to enjoy the natural soundscape. Avoid playing loud music.

10. Follow Regulations:

Know the Rules: Familiarize yourself with trial rules and observe them rigorously. This includes leash rules for dogs and seasonal trail closures.

By accepting the significance of conservation, engaging in volunteering opportunities, and practicing responsible hiking, you become an advocate for the preservation of our natural places. As we venture into the wide outdoors, let's do it with a strong feeling of stewardship, leaving behind just footprints and ensuring that the paths remain a sanctuary for those who follow in our footsteps.

8. HIKING EVENTS AND FESTIVALS

Welcome to the dynamic world of hiking events and festivals, where trails come alive with the spirit of exploration and fellowship. In this thorough guide, we'll dig into the yearly hiking events in Colorado, uncovering chances for exploration, learning, and celebration. Get ready to mark your calendars and join other outdoor enthusiasts in the fascinating arena of hiking events and festivals.

8.1 Annual Hiking Events in Colorado

A Year-Round Calendar of Adventure

1. Rocky Mountain National Park Winter Trails Day:

Location: Rocky Mountain National Park

Date: January

Highlights: Guided snowshoe walks and winter ecological programs for all ability levels.

2. Hiking Through History at Mesa Verde:

Location: Mesa Verde National Park

Date: April

Highlights: Guided walks explore the historic cliff dwellings and cultural history of Mesa Verde.

3. Colorado Springs Earth Day Hike:

Location: Various Trails in Colorado Springs

Date: April

Highlights: Celebrate Earth Day with community-led walks, educational events, and environmental awareness activities.

4. National Trails Day:

Location: Various Trails Across Colorado

Date: June (First Saturday)

Highlights: Nationwide celebration with scheduled treks, trail maintenance, and community gatherings.

5. Aspen Food & Wine Classic Hikes:

Location: Aspen

Date: June

Highlights: Combine dining experiences with trekking activities in the gorgeous Aspen scenery.

6. Leadville Trail 100:

Location: Leadville

Date: August

Highlights: Ultra trail events reaching 100 miles across the magnificent scenery of Leadville.

7. Colorful Colorado Fall Hikes:

Location: Various Trails Across Colorado

Date: September

Highlights: Guided treks to observe the gorgeous autumn colors around the state.

8. Winter Park Wipeout:

Location: Winter Park

Date: November

Highlights: A unique winter trail race involving obstacles and difficulties among the icy scenery.

9. Colorado Winter Trails Day:

Location: Various Trails Across Colorado

Date: January

Highlights: Introduction to winter activities including snowshoeing and cross-country skiing with free workshops and guided walks.

10. Hike with Santa:

Location: Various Trails Across Colorado

Date: December

Highlights: Family-friendly treks with Santa,

spreading festive happiness on the trails.

8.2 Hiking Festivals Calendar

Celebrating Nature, Adventure, and Community

1. Colorado Mountain Fest:

Location: Vail

Date: June

Highlights: Outdoor expos, adventure films, and guided treks to celebrate the mountain lifestyle.

2. Estes Park Mountain Festival:

Location: Estes Park

Date: July

Highlights: A multi-day event with guided walks, seminars, and outdoor activities for all ages.

3. Telluride Mushroom Festival:

Location: Telluride

Date: August

Highlights: While not strictly a hiking festival, it allows treks into the countryside to explore and learn about wild mushrooms.

4. Breckenridge Hiking & Nature Festival:

Location: Breckenridge

Date: August

Highlights: Guided walks, environmental workshops, and educational programs highlighting Breckenridge's unique landscapes.

5. Crested Butte Wildflower Festival:

Location: Crested Butte

Date: July

Highlights: Guided wildflower treks, photography workshops, and art displays honoring the magnificent floral variety.

6. Ouray Mountain Air Music Series:

Location: Ouray

Date: June to August (Weekly)

Highlights: Combine live music with treks in the San Juan Mountains during our summer concert series.

7. Silverton Alpine Marathon & 50K:

Location: Silverton

Date: July

Highlights: A trail race with spectacular alpine scenery in the San Juan Mountains.

8. Vail Outlier Festival:

Location: Vail

Date: September

Highlights: Adventure sports tournaments, gear expos, and guided treks to highlight outdoor interests.

9. Steamboat Stinger Trail Marathon & Half

Marathon:

Location: Steamboat Springs

Date: August

Highlights: Trail races across the magnificent Emerald Mountain environment.

10. Winter Trails Festival:

Location: Nederland

Date: February

Highlights: Snowshoe races, winter treks, and outdoor activities for all ages in the snowy surroundings of Nederland.

As you plan your hiking experiences, consider incorporating these events and festivals into your schedule. Whether you're attracted to instructional programmes, guided walks, or exuberant festivities, these events give you a terrific chance to interact with nature, other hikers, and the outdoor community. So, gear up and get ready to create unforgettable experiences on the trails of Colorado!

9. ACCOMMODATIONS AND SERVICES

Welcome to the world of luxury and convenience among the great outdoors. In this detailed guide, we'll cover the numerous lodging alternatives available to improve your hiking experience, ranging from camping beneath the stars to warm hotels and cabins. Additionally, we'll take a look at local communities and the resources they provide to guarantee your trek across Colorado's trails is not only exciting but also well-supported and pleasurable.

9.1 Camping Options
Underneath the Canvas and Stars
1. National Forest Campgrounds:

Locations: Throughout Colorado's National Forests

Highlights: Rustic campsites are tucked in

gorgeous natural settings, giving minimal facilities like fire pits and picnic tables.

2. State Park Campgrounds:

Locations: State Parks Across Colorado

Highlights: Campgrounds inside state parks provide a variety of facilities, from simple tent sites to RV hookups, along with access to park activities.

3. Dispersed Camping:

Locations: Designated Areas in National Forests and BLM Lands

Highlights: For those wanting a more private experience, scattered camping enables you to pitch up a tent in non-designated locations with few amenities.

4. Campgrounds Near Trailheads:

Locations: Proximity to Popular Trailheads

Highlights: Some campsites are conveniently positioned near trailheads, offering easy access to hiking routes.

5. Private Campgrounds:

Locations: Various Private Campgrounds Across the State

Highlights: Private campsites frequently provide a variety of facilities, from tent sites to RV connections, along with amenities like showers and laundry facilities.

9.2 Lodges and Cabins
Cozy Retreats in Nature's Embrace
1. National Park Lodges:

Locations: Within or Near National Parks

Highlights: Lodges provided by the National Park Service give pleasant lodgings with the additional bonus of being near great natural treasures.

2. Mountain Resorts:

Locations: Throughout Colorado's Mountainous Regions

Highlights: Resorts hidden in the mountains provide a luxury vacation with facilities such as spas, exquisite dining, and guided outdoor activities.

3. Cabin Rentals:

Locations: Various Scenic Locations

Highlights: Renting a cabin gives a pleasant, private escape with the amenities of home, frequently with cooking facilities and gorgeous surroundings.

4. Backcountry Huts:

Locations: Backcountry Areas in the Rockies

Highlights: Experience the appeal of backcountry

huts, giving a unique combination of rustic lodging and the excitement of being immersed in nature.

5. Bed and Breakfasts:

Locations: Historic Towns and Rural Settings

Highlights: Bed & Breakfast businesses provide a more intimate experience, generally in attractive settings with customized care.

9.3 Nearby Towns and Services
Hubs of Convenience and Charm
1. Estes Park:

Location: Gateway to Rocky Mountain National Park

Services: Accommodations, eating, outdoor gear stores, and tourist services.

2. Aspen:

Location: In the Heart of the Rockies

Activities: High-end lodgings, eating alternatives, art galleries, and outdoor leisure activities.

3. Breckenridge:
Location: Historic Mining Town
Services: Lodging, restaurants, shopping, and a bustling environment with cultural events.

4. Ouray:
Location: "Switzerland of America"
Services: Cozy inns, hot springs, eating, and access to gorgeous trails.

5. Salida:
Location: Along the Arkansas River
Services: Quaint lodgings, art galleries, and outdoor adventure outfitters.

6. Durango:
Location: Southwest Colorado

Services: Historic charm, accommodation, eating, and access to the Durango & Silverton Narrow Gauge Railroad.

7. Telluride:

Location: Surrounded by the San Juan Mountains
Services: Upscale accommodation, cultural events, and a bustling arts scene.

8. Grand Junction:

Location: Western Colorado
Services: Accommodations, wineries, and access to the Colorado National Monument.

9. Boulder:

Location: Foothills of the Rockies
Services: Diverse hotels, a thriving food scene, and outdoor leisure opportunities.

10. Fort Collins:

Location: Northern Colorado

Services: Breweries, hotels, and a busy downtown with shops and restaurants.

Conclusion

As you begin on your hiking excursion across Colorado, the broad choice of hotels and surrounding town amenities await, ensuring you have a comfortable and delightful time. Whether you prefer to camp under the stars, cuddle up in a mountain lodge, or visit attractive surrounding villages, the alternatives are as diverse as the sceneries that beautify the routes. So, suit up, find your perfect refuge, and get ready to build memories among the spectacular splendor of Colorado's great outdoors.

10. ADDITIONAL RESOURCES

Welcome to the last part of your complete guide to hiking in Colorado. In this part, we'll examine extra tools to augment your hiking experience, from suggested reading to online forums that build a feeling of camaraderie among outdoor lovers. We'll also give crucial emergency contacts to guarantee your safety on the trails. Let's dig into these helpful tools to improve your tour across Colorado's stunning landscapes.

10.1 Recommended Reading

Journey via Words: Books to Inspire and Inform

1. "Colorado's Fourteeners: From Hikes to Climbs" by Gerry Roach:

Overview: A thorough reference covering Colorado's iconic fourteeners, including insights into routes, trailheads, and the appeal of these high-altitude peaks.

2. "The Colorado Trail, 9th Edition" by Colorado Trail Foundation:

Overview: An official guidebook documenting the whole Colorado route, including maps, route descriptions, and critical information for thru-hikers and section hikers alike.

3. "Hiking Colorado's Front Range" by Bob D'Antonio:

Overview: Explore the Front Range with this handbook, which gives thorough information on routes, difficulty levels, and breathtaking vistas accessible from the Denver metropolitan region.

4. "Best Hikes with Dogs: Colorado" by Ania Savage:

Overview: Tailored for dog-loving hikers, this book highlights pet-friendly routes in Colorado, including information on leash requirements and canine safety.

5. "Colorado Wilderness Rides and Guides" by David A. Anderson:

Overview: A compilation of articles and tales, encapsulating the spirit of Colorado's outdoor experiences and offering inspiration for your excursions.

6. "100 Classic Hikes Colorado" by Scott Warren:

Overview: A selected collection of unique treks in Colorado, catering to all skill levels and tastes, with thorough trail descriptions and maps.

7. "The Ultimate Hiker's Gear Guide: Tools and Techniques to Hit the Trail" by Andrew Skurka:

Overview: A crucial resource for understanding and choosing the correct gear for your hiking experiences, published by famous long-distance hiker Andrew Skurka.

8. "Colorado's Best Wildflower Hikes: The High Country" by Pamela D. Irwin:

Overview: Delve into the brilliant world of

Colorado's wildflowers with this guide, identifying routes where you may observe nature's beautiful show.

10.2 Online Hiking Communities

Connecting Virtually: Joining Fellow Outdoor Enthusiasts

1. AllTrails:

Overview: A popular online platform and app where hikers exchange route reports, images, and suggestions. AllTrails offers a comprehensive database of trails, enabling you to find new routes and interact with a community of outdoor lovers.

2. Reddit - r/hiking:

Overview: Join the Reddit community devoted to hiking, where people exchange experiences, and route suggestions, and participate in conversations about all things connected to hiking.

3. Meetup:

Overview: Meetup gives a platform to connect with local hiking clubs and attend organized treks. It's a wonderful method to meet other hikers, particularly if you're new to the region or seeking like-minded folks.

4. Hiking Project:

Overview: A collaborative platform that includes extensive trail information, maps, and user evaluations. Hiking Project enables you to discover new paths and submit your own experiences.

5. Colorado Mountain Club:

Overview: Join the Colorado Mountain Club to engage with a community of outdoor enthusiasts. The group arranges treks, courses, and activities for members of all ability levels.

6. Facebook Groups:

Overview: Numerous Facebook groups concentrate on hiking in Colorado, allowing a forum to share experiences, seek advice, and interact with other hikers. Search for organizations relating to certain locations or hiking interests.

7. Instagram:

Overview: Explore the vivid world of hiking on Instagram by following hashtags such as #ColoradoHiking or #HikeColorado. Many hikers exchange gorgeous images, route suggestions, and insights on this visual platform.

10.3 Emergency Contacts

Safety First: Essential Numbers for Your Journey

1. Emergency Services:

Number: 911

Overview: In case of any emergency, phone 911 for rapid help from police, fire, or medical personnel.

2. Search and Rescue (Colorado Search and Rescue Association):

Number: Local emergency services

Overview: If you find yourself in need of emergency aid while trekking, calling local search and rescue authorities is vital. Save the local emergency services number for the region you'll be touring.

3. Poison Control Center:

Number: 1-800-222-1222

Overview: For aid with poison-related situations, including encounters with hazardous plants or animals.

4. Colorado State Parks Non-Emergency Number:

Number: Varies per park (see individual park websites)

Overview: For non-emergency circumstances at state parks, such as lost things or general queries.

5. National Park Service Information Line:

Number: 1-800-365-2267

Overview: For basic information on national parks in Colorado.

6. Local Ranger Stations:

Overview: Save the contact information for local ranger stations in the regions you want to walk. They may give vital information and support.

7. Colorado Trail Foundation (Non-Emergency):

Number: Varies (see the Colorado Trail Foundation website)

Overview: For non-emergency trail-related

queries and information.

Conclusion

As you go on your hiking experiences in Colorado, these extra materials are excellent companions. Whether you're seeking inspiration from suggested reading, connecting with other hikers in online groups, or ensuring your safety with emergency contacts, these tools are meant to enhance and secure your adventure. So, equip up, remain educated, and be ready to immerse yourself in the gorgeous scenery of Colorado's trails. Happy trekking!

CONCLUSION

Embarking on a Trail-Blazing Journey in Colorado
Congratulations, intrepid adventurer! You've
traveled the meandering paths of knowledge,
uncovering the treasures that lie in Colorado's
outdoor playground. As we approach the finish of
this thorough book, let's reflect on the adventure
we've begun and the thrill that lies ahead for your
hiking excursions.

Exploring Colorado's Diverse Terrain:

In our initial chapters, we revealed the incredible
variety that Colorado provides. From the
breathtaking peaks of the Rocky Mountains to the
red rock formations of Garden of the Gods, each
part of this state reveals a distinct narrative.
Whether you're attracted to alpine lakes, thick
woods, or broad meadows, Colorado's geography

encourages you to delve into a tapestry of natural treasures.

Safety First: Preparing for the Trail:

Our excursion also stressed the significance of safety. We went into planning factors, ensuring you chose the correct path for your ability level and the season. Safety recommendations and rules become your trusted friends, reminding you to respect nature, keep prepared, and build memories without sacrificing your well-being.

Trail Insights: From Peaks to Valleys:

Guided by our tour, you experienced some of Colorado's top hiking sites. From the legendary Rocky Mountain National Park to the tranquil Maroon Bells-Snowmass Wilderness, and the mesmerizing Garden of the Gods to the bizarre Great Sand Dunes National Park, the trails call with awe-inspiring vistas and distinct ecosystems.

Navigating Trails with Precision:

As a knowledgeable pioneer, you studied the ins and outs of trail profiles. We addressed difficulty levels, projected timings, elevation gain and loss, and highlighted important features and scenic places. Armed with this information, you're ready to pick paths that fit your tastes and talents.

Hiking with Companions: Family, Kids, and Pets:

For those with pint-sized companions or furry buddies, we dug into the art of family-friendly and pet-friendly hiking. Tips for hiking with children, family-friendly paths, and pet-friendly restrictions enable you to experience the pleasure of the trails with your loved ones.

Wilderness Survival Skills: Navigating Nature's Challenges:

Our journey traveled into the area of outdoor survival techniques, arming you with critical information. From navigation and map reading to first aid essentials, coping with animal interactions, and adopting Leave No Trace principles, you're now a well-prepared explorer ready to handle nature's challenges responsibly.

Trail Conservation & Stewardship:
With a heart committed to conservation, we studied conserving nature's treasures. Volunteering opportunities, ethical hiking habits, and a grasp of the Leave No Trace principles changed you into a steward of the trails, helping to the preservation of Colorado's natural beauty.

Accommodations and Services: Crafting Comfort in the Wilderness:

Our tour continued beyond the trails, leading you through a spectrum of lodging possibilities. Whether you enjoy camping beneath the stars, taking shelter in hotels and cabins, or visiting adjacent cities, Colorado provides a tapestry of alternatives to enhance your outdoor trip.

Additional Resources: Enhancing Your Hiking Experience:

In the last chapters, we introduced new materials to augment your trekking experience. Recommended reading, online hiking networks, and vital emergency contacts build a toolset to inspire, connect, and secure your safety amid the wide landscapes of Colorado.

Your Journey Continues:

As you stand at the crossroads of discovery, the trails of Colorado encourage you to strike forth. Each stride is a testimonial to the spirit of adventure that pulls you onward. Whether you're a seasoned hiker or a first-time adventurer,

Colorado's trails have a tale to tell, and you're now part of that narrative.

So, pack your stuff, strap on your hiking boots, and let the route unroll under your feet. Colorado's wilderness awaits, eager to expose its mysteries, uncover its beauty, and welcome you into its arms. May your trip be blessed with stunning sights, shared laughter with other hikers, and the peace that only nature can provide.

Thank you for joining our virtual excursion across the rugged beauty of Colorado's trails. As you journey out, may your way be lighted by the warm glow of discovery, and may each trek be a chapter in your particular adventure novel. Happy trails!

Made in the USA
Coppell, TX
05 June 2025

50388672R00056